My Inner Room

A Dialogue with My God

Barbara Laureles Valmeo

MY INNER ROOM

First edition. August 11, 2020.

ISBN: 979-8227016027

Written by Barbara Valmeo.

Table of Contents

To my dad, Jose S Laureles.

2016

AUGUST

"Remember that nothing is small in the eyes of God.
Do all that you do with love."
St. Therese of Lisieux

[1] August 7, 2016, Sunday (Adoration Chapel) The life of the church flows within you. Serve with a purpose. Allow yourself to see within you the good that you can do. Be at peace, for I am with you. Multiply My blessings by allowing others to work with you, for I am the giver of life, the life that goes abundantly through your works. Be at peace, for I am with you always. I love you, My child.

[2] August 13, 2016, Saturday (St. John Brebeuf, Niles IL, Adoration Chapel) Rejoice in My presence, for you chose to come before Me today. I am exalted by your thankful heart. I have bestowed special graces on you as you embark on this new journey ahead. I rejoice in you.

[3] August 19, 2016, Tuesday (Adoration Chapel) My will is for you to follow where I lead you. The path for you is arduous, but My light will guide you. Depend on Me, for I will always be at your side. Sit still and be at peace. The glory of the just awaits in My kingdom. Perseverance is the key to this glory. Rejoice, for I am your King!

[4] August 31, 2016, Wednesday (Adoration Chapel, 3:30 PM) The ministry set before you encompasses a myriad of ways to accomplish. Start with what is set before you. I will guide you on this journey. Your mind is busy planning for what I have already planned for you. Your duty is to Me before all else. You please Me with your obedience. My child, why fret about things only I have control over? Your willingness to fulfill My wishes is pleasing to Me. Be at peace.

SEPTEMBER

"Whether we realize it or not, prayer is the encounter of God's thirst with ours. God thirsts that we may thirst for him."
St. Augustine

[5] September 11, 2016, Sunday (Adoration Chapel) I speak to your heart, and all I ask is for you to listen. Listen to the one who calls you to join Me in My banquet. Your time will come when you will behold My face, but in the meantime, follow My footsteps. I will lead you towards the path that has been prepared for you. Your willingness to serve fills My heart with joy. The catch will be bountiful if you follow My way. Fill your heart with gladness so I can continue speaking My words to you. Your everlasting reward awaits.

[6] September 20, 2016, Tuesday (YMV Parking Lot, 10:00 AM) Listen to the rain. Let every drop remind you of the many blessings that await those who remain faithful. Listen. Only in stillness will you hear My voice. Thank you for heeding My call.

[7] September 25, 2016, Sunday (Adoration Chapel) Open your heart. Let Me gaze upon the goodness contained in it. Give Me your worries so that I can tame them. The pathway to heaven is tumultuous. Perseverance is the key to reaching your goal. I send individuals, holy ones, to make straight the path for you. With a trusting spirit, you will accomplish many tasks. Hear My voice. Listen. I am right beside you. My child, you are precious in My sight. My sweet, little lamb, trust in Me.

OCTOBER

"God speaks in the silence of the heart.
Listening is the beginning of prayer."
St. Theresa of Calcutta

[8] October 2, 2016, Sunday (Adoration Chapel, 8:30 PM) Poised for truth; the apostles went out to spread the truth, and I ask you to do the same. Trusting in Me alone, you can conquer the depths of the work set for those chosen ones. Brevity in words: our words will have the power to stir the hardened hearts. Prepare not too much, for My words will flow within you. My little one, you please Me so.

(9) October 13, 2016, Thursday (Our Lady of Bethesda Chapel, MD) In you, I see a child whom I love so much. Stay close to Me, and together, we will discover My Father's will.

[10] October 15, 2016, Saturday (Our Lady of Bethesda Chapel, MD) Believe in Me. The depths of your love for Me resounds like a gong in heaven. I hear you, My child. Hear Me in return as I speak in the deepest recesses of your being. You will be My feet on earth. I will take you to places where My lost sheep awaits. Place your hope in Me. I will not let you down. Go, My little shepherd. Thank you for heeding My call.

[11] October 30, 2016, Sunday (Adoration Chapel) My love has no boundaries. I want you to learn to love everyone that I send your way. Do not choose who to love because you are all loved by My Father. Open your heart to Me that I may fill it with My everlasting love, a love that will be visible to the hardened hearts. It is My love that will calm your fears. It is I alone that you need, My words alone that you should listen to. My sheep, hear My voice, for I will never forsake you. You are precious in My sight.

[12] October 23, 2016, Sunday (Adoration Chapel) The love of a mother is not bound by space and time. My Mother sends Her love. Your words and prayers are being heard. Remove your doubts. In its place, harbor trust. You sense the urgency. Times ahead, I only know. Prepare the way for many. Count not what you can do. The bounty of the catch will surprise you. Worry not. Press on. Remain faithful. You are loved.

NOVEMBER

"I would never want any prayer that would
not make the virtues grow within me."
St. Teresa of Avila

[13] November 27, 2016, Sunday (Adoration Chapel) I took you out from the hands of your oppressors to bring you the fullness of your servitude to the Father. You are called to the greater task of walking the path that few people have trodden. I know, I feel, I see you. I have prepared you for the task ahead. Look for Me at every bend, every corner, every crossroads ahead. I am always beside you to be your guide, your beacon of light. Stay close to Me, and I will do the same. The pattern in which you are serving Me has changed, but in this way, you can bring back to Me those who have lost their way. I choose you to bring light to others. Where other people forgo, you are to go. I have bestowed gifts upon you that others cannot attain in their lifetime. You, My child, have shown Me your love for Me and My Father. Go and show forth this love to all My children that We will send your way. Rejoice, for I rejoice in you.

DECEMBER

*"Prayer is the inner bath of love into which the
soul plunges itself."*
St. Jean Marie Baptiste Vianney

[14] December 14, 2016, Sunday (Adoration Chapel) Beginning to forgive is a step toward healing. I know the hurt you went through, and yet I allowed it to happen. Why? For your good, for the good of your soul. You see, pride has crept into your work. I needed to take you out of that ministry to keep you from falling deeper into prideful service. You are to be Our example of hope to those whom I will send you. Accept truths as they come. Learn from Me, the source of all knowledge. There's more to come. Receive the graces I have reserved just for you. Just keep your eyes on Me. I love you, My child. You please Me.

2017

JANUARY

"A humble soul does not trust itself,
but places all its confidence in God."
St. Faustina Kowalska

[15] January 23, 2017, Monday (Adoration Chapel, 12:10 PM) Your obedience pleases Me. My Church is on the verge of ruins, and My children are in peril. Consecrate your work to My Mother's Immaculate Heart. She will, in turn, bless it to bear much fruit. Come to Me with all your concerns. The path ahead seems treacherous. Cling to Me, and I will carry you across each hurdle. Your mission is to bring to Me My children who are so lost in this world. Spend more time with Me. I miss you.

[16] January 29, 2017, Sunday (Adoration Chapel) Listen, My child. The world clamors for your attention. Listen. Listen only to My voice, for I alone can make straight your path. When you come before Me, allow yourself to rest in My presence. I, too, long for you.

FEBRUARY

"The prayers of the Saints in heaven and of the just on earth are a perfume which never will be lost."
St. Padre Pio

[17] **February 5, 2017, Sunday** (Adoration Chapel) Find the time to commune with Me. I desire for you to begin your days praising Me. Like a river that flows to the sea, so should your path be directed to Me. I already know what is in your heart. Connect with My heart, for I wish to bring you peace and joy. Direct your gaze at Me constantly. Listen only to My voice. Your joys and pains and troubles and strife, I would lovingly take as a pleasing sacrifice. Press on, My child, press on. You are loved.

[18] **February 6, 2017, Monday** (Prayer Room) Waste not any minute of the precious time I give you each day on idle things. Praise God through your works of charity. Only then will your time be wisely spent. Open your heart, mind, and soul to allow the Holy Spirit to hover over you all day long. You are precious in My sight.

[19] **February 8, 2017, Wednesday** (Prayer Room) The distance between the good and the bad, only I can measure. What is important is that you do not forget those in between. The souls in purgatory long for your prayers. Do not forget to quench their thirst with your prayers. Like you, they long to be with Me. Offer this day for them. Fear not the enemy. Focus

on doing only My will. Yes, you will encounter contradictions. Perseverance, My child, will be the key. Prayers can bring down the walls between My will and others' will. Look for Me in every circumstance you will face. I am always here for you. Trust in Me alone. Hold My hand, cling to Me always.

[20] **February 9, 2017, Thursday** (Prayer Room) My words come to you in the silence of your heart. Spend more time with Me in still-ness, for I wish to speak with you. Time spent with Me is never a waste, for I give you hope for the day. Go forth. I have bestowed graces upon you for your walk of faith today. Come to Me. Hold My hand. I am always here for you. You are loved.

[21] **February 10, 2017, Friday** (Prayer Room) The Father's love pours down freely to those whose hearts are open to receive them. Continue to open your heart to Him so that His love can shine through you to others. The duty placed on your shoulders reflects His trust in you. We thirst for the souls who have gone astray. Gather them back to the flock. I am with you always, My little child. Trust in Me. I love you.

[22] **February 12, 2017, Sunday** (Adoration Chapel) Fear not. The strength to overcome obstacles comes from Me. Obstacles and hurdles that come your way are merely distractions from the enemy because your work is very important in rebuilding My Church. Recognize that all I ask is your willingness to do My will and the rest will fall into place because I desire so. My lost sheep are scattered. Tend to them. Many will be lost but some are just waiting for the right time, for the right person to come to their rescue. I am saddened by the indifference shown to Me by My children. The world has turned against Me. I, who came to save them. My child, persevere. Have faith in the one who sends

you out into the field. The vast land offers many opportunities to pluck the harvest. Stay strong, hold on. I will be your guide. Come to Me always. I delight in you, My little lamb. Rest now in My presence.

[23] **February 14, 2017, Tuesday** (Prayer Room) Rejoice in the Lord! Teach My children to rejoice in Me! Dependence on Me is necessary for our trusting and loving relationship. I belong to you, you belong to Me. I desire all My children to come into My kingdom. If they only knew My heart, they would find a heart full of love, unconditional love, for all. The saints knew that love. Pray that you can attain the depths of their love for Me. I love you My little lamb. Rejoice in Me!

[24] **February 15, 2017, Wednesday** (Prayer Room) Allow yourself to love even those who disappoint you. When things do not go as planned, know that I am holding your hand. Persevere. No one can see and feel what you are going through but Me. I know things before they happen. Trust in Me, the Potter, for I am molding you along the way. Consider looking out of your comfort zone. There are people in your life who I have placed to help you. Worry not. We are watching over you. Come to Me always. I am here.

[25] **February 16, 2017, Thursday** (Prayer Room) Stay close to My heart and I will give you rest. The journey seems so long but the roads you take must be traveled by you. You alone have these roads been designed for. Again, I tell you, persevere. I hear your thoughts; I see your actions. Fear not the test. Rejoice in the glory to come. Always focus on Me. The uncertainty of the future should give you only hope and not fear. Search for My face in every situation you encounter. You will soon realize that I am always here waiting for you to call out My name. My dear

child, you are loved more than you will ever know. Continue the journey. Enjoy the walk with Me.

[26] February 17, 2017, Friday (Prayer Room) Reflect on the "Sermon on the Mount." In it you will find ways to calm the storm, to combat the enemy. I desire for you to always allow Me to lead the way. Come to Me before making any decisions, especially concerning your relationship with others. You see problems, I have the solutions. We created you with special gifts and talents. Use them with My accord. You can bring fruition to the work entrusted to you only if your heart is set upon pleasing Me. Pray, pray always. You are loved, My little lamb. Go forth. I am with you.

[27] February 18, 2017, Saturday (Prayer Room) Direct your gaze at the one who has singled you out amongst many to capture the hearts of My children. I see your frustration. Compliance with My words are never easy for many because the world has a tight grip on them. Do not be like them for you belong to Me. Courage will take you to many unexpected places. I will give you the strength to overcome challenges and pitfalls along the way. Look closely around the people you encounter. By My grace, you are to recognize those who can give you a helping hand. Do not offend anyone who is blocking your way but rather, show them love and respect. Only through love can one change one's disposition. Carry your task with only love in your heart, for hatred has no room in My Father's glory. Enjoy the ride. Be a faithful student. You are loved, My little lamb. How precious you are to Me.

[28] February 19, 2017, Sunday (Prayer Room) My words from the past, I speak to you today. Listen. Let My words be your guide. Holiness can be attained when your heart is in tune with

Mine. The needs of others come before you. Bring them all to Me so I, in turn, can bring them to the Father. These prayers are treasures in heaven. We delight in them. The abundance of My provisions to those who generously give to others, no one can fathom. I can see through man's hearts. Your good intentions, I know. Trust in My Divine Providence. I will never forsake you. Cry not for the world, My dear child. My love flows to all My children, though many chose to gaze in the opposite direction. They will be punished in time. But those who remain faithful, I will gather soon. My mercy abounds if only My children will ask for it. Direct your gaze at Me. My love overflows for you.

[29] **February 20, 2017, Monday** (Prayer Room) Condemn not those who in any way oppress you. They, too, are My children. Pray, pray that hearts may welcome Me. The sorrow I feel for the loss of many is unbearable. I, your God, have immense love for all. How I grieve for them! Console Me with your continuous openness to My promptings. You, My child, will show the way for many. Persist in doing My will. I will be holding your hand on every journey I take you. Sing only of My goodness, for I delight in you.

[30] **February 21, 2017, Tuesday** (Prayer Room) The joy in My heart overflows when My children gather in prayer. Heaven rejoices at the sound of prayers. My Father and I share the joy as the Holy Spirit dwells on those who exalts us. Pray always, My child. The time you spend with Me in prayer brings you closer to My heart. Delight in the time you spend with Me because I delight in you. Consider bringing My words to others. The world needs to know what is in My heart. I desire for men to grow in love with Me. I thirst for their love. My child, how you please Me with your obedience. Yes, I talk with you in silence and at your

busy times. The more you will listen, the more I will speak. Dear child, you belong to Me.

[31] February 22, 2017, Wednesday (Prayer Room) Motherhood is a sacred duty. A Mother's devotion to her children brings Me joy. Keep your eyes on Me as you balance your daily duties. I give you each day with plans I have set for you. Trust in Me. Nothing is impossible if you allow Me to hold your hand. Include Me in every thought, decision, or action. In this way, your every footstep will lead to Me. Thank you for spending time with Me. You are loved.

[32] February 23, 2017, Thursday (Prayer Room) Bring to Me all your worries, for they just clutter your mind. Your complete trust in Me can dispel any lingering worry. I hear all your prayers. The answers have already been set in motion, so why do your thoughts keep going back to your concerns? Trust in Me always. Am I not your God? Devotion to My Mother I keep close to My heart. Oh, how She loves all Her children. She weeps for every soul who goes astray. She mourns the loss of souls to hell. For every tear She sheds, I, too, shed My tears as well. How I love My Mother! How She longs to enfold Her children in Her arms! (Adoration Chapel) The heart that burns with love for God can illuminate this dark, fallen world. I desire for men to constantly be in awe of My Father's love. It is basking in this love that will enable one to defeat the enemy. Love alone should rule in one's heart. My dear child, continue to love.

[33] February 24, 2017, Friday (Prayer Room) I, the Just One, see the plight of His people. It is easy to follow the road to despair when one walks alone. My light awaits. Learning to depend on Me is a hard lesson to master. Oftentimes, pain and suffering mask My call. My dear children, come to Me, depend on Me, trust in Me. The narrow path ahead is daunting. You must travel this path to get to know Me. I never said it would be easy. Life, as you know it, is so minute compared to eternity. Keep on walking with Me. The strength to follow Me is a grace I bestow on those who trust in Me. Recognize My hand in problems, joys, and roadblocks along the way. When you do, the weight that you carry will be lighter and easier. Then and only then is your walk in life bearable. Why trudge along when you can fly with Me? Come, come to My banquet, My children. I am waiting.

[34] **February 26, 2017, Sunday** (Adoration Chapel, 9:30 PM) Utter My name with love. Speak My words with love. Come to Me with love. This I ask of you, My child. Praise My Holy Name with gladness in your heart. Abandon your worries behind when you come before Me. You already know what I am asking you to do. Your heart knows My words. Do not refute what you already know is coming from Me. Worry not. Trust in Me. You know it is I speaking to you. Again, listen attentively to Me. Do you have control over tomorrow? Do not I always come to your aid? A willing heart is all I ask of you. [Address your concerns with Deacon Bill. Do not hinder your openness with your self-doubt. You know it is Me.] Be attentive to what your heart is telling you. The more you offer your heart to Me, the more I will show you My desires for you. The Holy Spirit will direct your ways. Pay attention. There is more to come. Do you trust Me, My little lamb? Then, why worry? You know what to do. My blessings, I shower upon you, My dear, dear child.

[35] **February 27, 2017, Monday** (Prayer Room, 7:00 AM) Your thoughts are many. Serenity is obtained by whispering My name whenever you feel overwhelmed. Even on a hard journey,

whisper My name, and you will see how it will dispel your worries. Find comfort in knowing that I am always beside you. Pursue holiness. Your thoughts and actions should only reflect My goodness. Grace, though unseen, can be felt by those whose hearts are open to receive them. Again, pursue holiness. Come to Me when you are weary. I, who give everlasting life, also give everlasting peace and joy. This day, like all other days, is anointed. Go forth and share My blessing to others. You are loved.

[36] February 28, 2017, Tuesday (Prayer Room, 7:00 AM) Dwell not in the past. Each day brings new hope for the future. So many of My children only see darkness ahead because they have forgotten how brightly My light shines. Bring My light to those whose days are bleak and cloudy. They have no hope; they have no God. How I long for My children to recognize Me once more. The singing birds, the blooming flowers, the clouds that cover the sun to give shade, the blowing wind...they all should be a gentle reminder of the God who loves. The enemy is strong because hearts have allowed him entry. Oh, My child, bring them back to Me. I will bless all your efforts to help this fallen world. Look to Me for guidance. You are to follow My promptings alone. This time you spend with Me is enough to conquer whatever troubles the enemy has set for you. You are under Our protection. Be at peace. My little lamb, you are loved.

MARCH

"Prayer is still a little known means; however, it is the most effective way to reestablish peace in our souls because it allows us to get ever closer to God's love."
St. Maximilian Kolbe

[37] March 1, 2017, Ash Wednesday (Prayer Room, 7:00 AM) To teach about Me is a noble act of charity. To love God with your whole heart is likened to being in heaven, where love abounds. My children, come to Me. Your Father awaits to show forth His love. Come. Follow the path I laid out for you, the road less traveled, Yes, that is the one. For this road always leads to Me. Follow Me, My child, for your reward is greater than you could even imagine. Compassion for others is needed on this road. Focus not on your own will but on Mine. As you walk along this path, the more you take notice of others, the more you will see Me. Come, take My hand. I will walk with you on this journey. Follow the inspirations I send your way. Listen with the heart of a child. You are precious in My sight.

[38] March 2, 2017, Thursday (Prayer Room, 9:00 PM) Dream big. Do not limit yourself to evangelizing only those around you. Look at the big picture, for what you do today will have an impact tomorrow. Do not make temporary plans. When you set things in motion, ensure their permanence. You are to plant seeds where you are now, but be always ready to move on. Many of My children are thirsty for the truth. Reach out to them. You will learn as you travel the road. I will guide you. Remain open to receive My graces. You alone must travel the path that I designed for you. Many people stop and, thus, never really discover the many surprises I have set along the way. Again, pursue holiness. It is the only way you can attain the glory in My Kingdom. Do you long for Me, My child?

[39] **March 3, 2017, Friday** (Prayer Room, 8:20 AM) Think of Me when you pray. Do not mumble your words. Say your prayers with love. It is then that you commune with Me. Pray with gladness in your heart. I delight in a joyful heart. Although I know everything in your life, tell Me anyway. Do not best friends tell each other's secrets? Just the same, let your conversation with Me be as lively or sullen as you would a good friend. My words I desire for you to share. Deaf ears will not hear them, but the just will. Be not afraid to face your detractors. Keep planting seeds. That's all I ask of you. Plant seeds. Live today as if it were your last. In this way, no time is wasted, no time is lost. Your devotion to My Mother is of utmost importance. She, too, is pleased with your obedience. Her mantle of protection is around you. My dear child, how you please Us so!

[40] **March 4, 2017, Saturday** (Prayer Room, 2:00 PM) Speak up, My people, speak up. The grace of God is abounding on those who spread the truth. Collectively work together to raise once more the Church, the one true Church that I have firmly established on earth. Consider pouring out your time and effort in ways that are pleasing to God alone. Enough time has been lost by many who choose to disregard the needs of others, the needs of the Church. Why do you hesitate? The Holy Spirit is in each one of you who has been baptized and confirmed. Do you

doubt the power of the Paraclete? He lives in you. Allow Him to live through you. Your works are what I desire. Amongst all the other tasks you engage in, your work for the Church should be your focus. Live each day serving God first. Nothing else matters because I will take care of it. Dispose of worries and fears. The Holy Spirit will arm you in battle. It is time. My children, hear Me. The Lord, your God, is pleading. Speak up.

[41] March 5, 2017, Sunday (Prayer Room, 7:00 AM) Be assured of My grace every time you serve Me. The seed you plant, I will water. The ripple effect of your efforts you may not see, but trust that you are not working in vain. The beauty of a willing servant, only the master knows. I see through your struggles; I see through your heart. I am here. I am always at your side. The world exists because of Me. Live, then, according to My will alone. Your here and now is with Me. Stay close to Me. Worship Me and love Me. Let your heart overflow with gladness. The gushing of blessings from heaven will be upon you. Believe in Me.

[42] March 7, 2017, Tuesday (Prayer Room, 7:00 AM) Capture the hearts of many with your truthfulness and kindness. Trust that I guide your works of charity. Depend on Me, for I have the power to break down any barriers in your path. Your life is a gift, treasure it. (It is My Mother's Blue Mantle that protected you. Thank Her.) A thankful heart gives Us absolute joy. Cherish your life. Spend your days loving Me. Fill your days with thoughts of Me. Occupy your time getting to know Me. I am the giver of life. I desire to spend time with you. I assure you of your place in heaven if you follow Me. Come to Me, My child. Hold My hand today and every day. Your master awaits. You are loved.

*My daughter and I were in an accident on March 5, 2017, 5:45 PM

[43] March 8, 2017, Wednesday (Family Room,10:30 AM) Leave things undone today for tomorrow. Remember, they are your plans, not Mine. Make the most of each day by basking in the graces I shower upon you when you spend time with Me. Take care not to get caught in the web of activities spun by the enemy designed to take you away from Me. Beware of his traps, for they are many. Follow Me on the road to salvation. When you rest, I, too, will rest with you. Allow Me to take your hand and lead the way. Do not go before Me lest you stumble in the dark. Remember, I will travel with you to the ends of the earth only if you allow Me to. I am always here for you, My child. How I love you so!

[44] March 10, 2017, Friday (Prayer Room, 8:00 AM) The promise of tomorrow I will bring to you. Hold fast to doing works of charity. The more you share My love, the more love I will pour into your heart. Be careful not to boast of your good deeds. The Father and I know all your works. Stay humble and serve with love. Consult with the Holy Spirit. He will guide your thoughts and actions. Focus on following our will, and all your endeavors will be fruitful. Be quick to pardon those who oppose you. They are merely ploys by the enemy to distract you. Focus on Me. I will lead the way. Your concerns for your family, I already know. Trust that as you serve Me, I will take care of them. Am I not the source of all goodness? They are all precious to Me. I take care of all. Come to My, My child. Come. You are loved.

[45] March 11, 2017, Saturday (Prayer Room, 4:00 PM) Mend your ways. Look at everyone with love. Watch your thoughts so that, though unspoken, they are not judging others. Remember that we can hear your thoughts. Be aware of your actions lest they be self-centered and unjust. Bless others with your smile and genuine concern. Your deeds have more weight when done with love. Concern yourself not with how you will accomplish tasks, but rather, keep your gaze at Me. When you focus on pleasing Me, everything else will fall into place. Worry not about tomorrow, otherwise, you will miss the opportunities I have set before you today. My children are so self-absorbed that they take no notice of the blessings I have scattered around them. The sunlight, the birds' chatter, the cold breeze, and the morning dew...are gentle reminders to acknowledge Me. Why do so many ignore Me, the God who created the world? Participate in My saving grace by your conformity to My will. Tribulations along the way are set to teach you virtues necessary for your salvation. Persist in doing what is good and just. I am right beside you always. Come to Me, My child. Your master awaits.

[46] **March 12, 2017, Sunday** (Adoration Chapel, 8:30 PM) Refresh your soul by meditating on My words. The more you dig deeper into the mysteries I left behind, the more I will reveal My heart's desire for you. Complete union with Me can be obtained through the sacraments and in living out the gospel. My words apply to all generations. I am still the God of the past, of today and tomorrow. I convey the same message throughout man's history. Open your hearts so that you may hear My voice. The darkness that is upon this world you should not fear. I will always be your guiding light. Look ahead, for I am there before you. Do not look back for what is in your past I already have forgotten. An eternity with Me should be your life's goal, for I wish you no lesser reward. Praise only My name. Seek only My face. Follow only My voice. I will lead you home. I love you, dear child.

[47] **March 13, 2017, Monday** (Prayer Room, 8:00 AM) Show compassion and tenderness to all My children. In this way, My love will shine from you through them. So many are weary and downtrodden because they do not know Me. Find joy in every circumstance you are in. Pain and suffering, which so many of My children are afraid of, are given to those who are called to offer more. Giving up one's comfort and desires for Me is a source of our joy. Today comes with more surprises. Keep Me in your thoughts, and I will show them to you. Offer every thought, action, and word to Me, and I, in turn, will show you the beauty of being one with Me. I wish to be included in your day, for I am continually watching you. Say My name and know that I am with you always. My love goes to all My children.

[48] **March 15, 2017, Wednesday** (Prayer Room, 9:30 PM) The lives touched by a gentle spirit are known only by Us. Be kind and caring to all who come your way. You never know when a hardened heart is stirred by your actions. You may never find out how, unbeknown to you, a stranger receives a seed you planted. All of these we nurture so that the seed will grow roots. Keep moving on, knowing that you are guided by the Holy Spirit. I can see your troubled heart. Without Me, you can do nothing. But with Me, trust that all your duties will be completed in time. Do I not always make time for you? Just the same, make time for Me. Resist the temptation to worry. The plans I have for you are hard only if you let go of My hand. Take each day as an adventure where your companion is the Creator of the Universe. In this way, worry will not have any room because, in its place, you will have the freedom to enjoy My company. How I love you, My child! Come and go on an adventure with Me.

[49] March 17, 2017, Friday (Prayer Room, 6:00 AM) Listen to My words. The narrow path ahead seems laden with thorns. The soul is made pure through suffering. Tell My children to persevere. An eternal life with Me is obtained through works of love despite trials and hardships. Persevere, My children, persevere. I never abandon anyone on the road to salvation. Do not let go of Me. Keep your focus on the end goal, for then and only then will your burden be lighter. I do not ever want any of My children to go astray. I walk with you, laugh with you, cry with you, love with you. Stay close to Me. I am always here beside you. Remember, the Lord, your God, loves you.

[50] March 19, 2017, Sunday (Adoration Chapel, 8:45 PM) Speak My words to those whom I send your way. You can recognize them by listening to Me. My way of speaking comes in different ways, thus, keep your heart in tune with Mine. It is then that your actions, too, will be in tune with My desires. Free yourself from doubt and fear. How can you go on the journey ahead if your heart is full of trepidation? Unload your burdens to Me. I take care of My sheep. Renew your faith every day. With each passing day, come closer to Me. I do not walk away from My children. They walk away from Me. Oh, how I long to bring them to My sheepfold. If only all will hear My call. My child, walk with Me. Comfort Me with your company. I am calling you.

[51] March 20, 2017, Monday (Prayer Room, 8:30 AM) As you look at the day ahead, keep your eyes on the one who is constantly at your side. There is no task we cannot do together. The daunting list of work does not all have to be done today. I give you every day with new opportunities, new ideas, new possibilities. Look forward to each new day because I am ever present in your life. Gather your thoughts and bring them to Me. Let Me direct them towards doing the will of My Father. As always, all is up to you. It is your choice which direction to go. Let your faith guide your works. With a thankful heart, spend the day with Me. I wish to be a part of your day. I wish to be loved by you. Your every thought, word, or deed offered to Me is truly a sweet sacrifice of love. Stay close to Me, My child. You are dearly loved.

[52] March 22, 2017, Wednesday (Prayer Room, 11:00 PM) Once again, I tell you, part ways with this fallen world. Live according to My will and not the world's. When you set yourself apart for Me, the more you will see the flaws offered by the enemy. Stay close to Me so I, myself, can steer you away from danger. Detach yourself from the needs of the flesh. There is nothing in this world worthy of praise but Me. Wisdom comes from God. Ask for the gift of wisdom to help you navigate the road that leads to Me. My sweet lamb, call on Me alone. I am here for you.

[53] March 23, 2017, Thursday (Prayer Room, 7:00 AM) Perform your duties with love. The needs of your family should come first. Although I ask you to serve others for Me, your domestic church comes first. The monotony of your responsibilities seems insignificant to you. Performed with love and offered to Me, this seemingly unimportant work is pleasing to Me. Your husband and children are My children, too. I am pleased with every sacrifice you make on behalf of any of My children. My mercy abounds to those who ask. It gives Me great joy when My children come to Me. All you need to do is ask. I am a God who loves all. Come to Me. I have so much to give. My heart overflows with love and compassion. My blessings I do not hold out to those who ask. Come, My children, come. The heavenly choir awaits the homecoming of the just. Come.

[54] March 24, 2017, Friday (Prayer Room, 7:00 AM) Tenderness and compassion I ask of you to give to your brothers and sisters. I have shown you how to love one another. Follow My lead. Take notice of the people around you. So many of them know about Me. A few of them know Me. Conquer the world by living just as I lived...loving all, giving all, calling all to God. Despite the contradictions of many, persist in doing what is good and just. Be kind to those who are unkind. Be mellow to those who are harsh. Be truthful to those who distort the truth. Love the unloved. Look beyond the people around you. Many of My children are just waiting to be touched by genuine concern. Go to them, for they are ready for harvesting. Go, My dear child. Go and touch others with My love. My blessings are with you.

[55] March 26, 2017, Sunday (Prayer Room, 8:00 AM) Praise the Lord, your God, always. It is easy to do so if you recognize the love that I poured into everything I created for you. See the wondrous things I have done because I, too, want to please you. My children, how I love you so! Courage is a gift I bestow on those who are willing to heed My call. Speak of My love to everyone you come across with. Be My voice. Do not be afraid to proclaim My words. Speak for Me, for I wish for My children to hear Me. Counsel the spiritually thirsty. So many wander this world full of necessary provisions, but their souls are in the desert, parched. Reach out to them, My child, for there are many. My heart longs to see them come back to My flock. Your obedience consoles My heart. Thank you for your time. You are lovely in My sight.

[56] March 27, 2017, Monday (Prayer Room, 10:30 PM)
Commitment to your duties to God is of utmost importance. Although you may contradict everything this world dictates, stand your ground and follow the narrow path. Too many people ignore the inner voice that leads them to Me. The world has become deaf to My call. Pour your heart into pleasing Me. I cannot force My children to love Me, but still, I love. My heart yearns for My children to love Me back. Hear Me, My sheep, your shepherd is calling. Come back to Me.

APRIL

"Prayer is true rest."
St. Francis of Assisi

[57] **April 1, 2017, Saturday** (Prayer Room, 7:00 AM) Seek to live the truth. God's image has been distorted to attract more of My children to the false promises of the evil one. Be that one who calls people out of darkness. Bring them to My light. How can My children hear Me in this noisy world? Clothe yourself in silence, for in detachment from the world will you hear My voice and feel My love. Comfort Me with your obedience to My will. Peace is what I give to those who follow My lead. Do not resist the work of the Holy Spirit, for he desires to commune with you. Your footsteps must be directed at gathering My lost sheep, who are being carried away by the tide. Bring them back to Me, My dear one. Do not be afraid. Just be willing to serve Me. How I grieve the loss of My children! If they only know how I long for them! My precious Mother cannot bear My sufferings, and so She suffers, too. Listen attentively, for there is much work to be done. Just be obedient to My call. I, the Lord, your God, dwell in your heart. You have nothing to fear.

[58] **April 2, 2017, Sunday** (Prayer Room, 8:00 AM) Come to Me for rest. Your mind is too busy planning the pursuit of worldly things. Rest in My presence and feel My love. Calm your thoughts by thinking of Me. Your fears and worries, I will replace

with peace and joy. Rest, My child, rest with Me. Compliance with My Commandments, I ask. Teach about My desire for all to join Me in My kingdom. These commands are meant to purify one's soul and gain entry to heaven. Plant the seed of the desire to come home to Me. The eternal happiness which I have prepared is indescribable. I wish for all My children to attain holiness. Forgive each other for every offense, even if though it may be so minute. Do not carry around burdens of guilt and shame. These effects of sins will only slow you down on your journey. Confess, repent, and follow Me. Although the road may be treacherous, defy the enemy, and I will equip you with graces to navigate your path. Again, I say to you, direct your gaze at Me, your end goal. I am waiting. My child, you are loved. Thank you for spending time with Me. I enjoy your company.

(10:00 AM) Partake of My goodness by being open to receiving them. I shower My blessings all day long to those who are waiting for them. Seek My face amongst the crowd. Find me in the clouds, the blue sky, the treetops, the blowing wind, and the smallest flower. I am ever present in your lives. See Me. Preserve the truth by living it. Consciousness of the well-being of all would lead you to true love for all. Judging others will be difficult if you truly love. Finding faults would be impossible if you only see the goodness that is innate in all My children. Pursue holiness. My children, I love you all!

*Received while getting ready for church and during the ride to church.

[59] **April 3, 2017, Monday** (Prayer Room, 11:00 PM) Plant seeds of hope. Tomorrow seems bleak to too many of My children. Let them get to know Me. Teach them about Me. Reach out to them and show them how to find Me. Desperation

comes from turning away from My light. I offer eternal joy, and yet, so many prefer the fleeting joy on earth. How this saddens Me! My children, let Me be a part of your lives. I gave you life so that one day we will be together once more in My kingdom. Come to Me. My mercy awaits those who ask for them. Mend your ways. My arms are open and waiting to enfold you, just come to Me. I am waiting.

[60] **April 4, 2017, Tuesday** (YMV Parking Lot, 9:00 AM) Practice the virtue of patience. Why do you insist on making things happen now? Remember that your time is not My time, your thoughts are not My thoughts. Do not hinder My plans by coming up with your own. Do not go ahead of Me because, without Me, your journey will be more difficult. Allow Me to walk with you. Why travel alone when you can have the company of the one who created you? Just like a puzzle, allow Me to unfold My plans at My pace. Understanding the how and when is not what I ask of you. Patience, perseverance, and trust in your Lord are of utmost importance in your walk of faith. Do not forget to hold My hand. Let Me go with you as you traverse the path that I specifically designed for you. I wish to be a part of your every step, your every thought, your every action. My child, how precious you are to Me!

[61] **April 5, 2017, Wednesday** (Prayer Room, 11:00 PM) Rest your weary souls by spending time with Me. I am here waiting to hear about your worries, concerns, joys, and accomplishments. Am I not your Father? I wish to hear from you. Whisper My name.

[62] **April 6, 2017, Thursday** (Prayer Room, 10:00 PM) Treasure the time you spend with your children. I treasure every minute of the time you spend with Me. Human love is a strong

emotion. The Father's love is simply unexplainable. The depth of My Father's love for all is unthinkable in the human mind. Tune out the voice of this world so you can hear Me. So many tasks demand your attention. When you come before Me, leave these thoughts behind. The world does not stop with undone tasks. I, who give time, will allow you to finish your list in My own time. Relax and keep Me company. I am always with you.

[63] **April 7, 2017, Monday** (Prayer Room, 10:00 PM) Always think of the goodness of the Lord. Your life's circumstances are allowed by God, the Father. It is your response to His will that will determine the outcome. Trust in Us. Remember that the acceptance of the Father's will will always lead to a deeper communion with Him. My Father allows suffering for your salvation. I will never leave your side. My Mother is at your side. What are you to fear? Have peace in your heart. Trust in Me. My child, do you not know how much we love you? Rest now.

*We found out today that my daughter and I might have a concussion from our accident on March 5.

[64] **April 8, 2017, Saturday** (Bedroom, 7:00 PM) Ponder My words. Silence is a sure way to hear Me. Detach yourself from the world to hear Me. I have much to say. Listen attentively. Just listen. Release your worries to Me. The time to hear is now. Clarity of mind comes after a peaceful encounter with Me. Do not delay, for I wish to meet with you. Slowly surrender your thoughts to Me. I, in turn, have much more to share with you. Meet Me on this journey. I have so much to share.

[65] **April 9, 2017, Sunday** (Adoration Chapel, 11:30 AM) Conform your will with My will. The more you surrender yourself, the more blessings I will pour upon your soul. I need you to take My hand and not let go. Immerse yourself in My

words, and in it, you will find treasures you will not find elsewhere. Do you trust Me? Would you like Me to take you on a journey? Come, My child. Your Father awaits. Deep conversion means letting go of control and allowing Me to be your sole guide. Relieve yourself of the burdens placed by the world on your shoulders. Follow Me with full abandon. I will not let you down. Meditate on the path to salvation. I will be there to show you the way. Come now. Come.

[66] **April 10, 2017, Monday** (Prayer Room, 9:00 AM) Return to the one who loves you. Strip yourself of worldly desires. Clothe yourselves with treasures from heaven. My graces I freely give to those whose lives reflect God's love. On the cross, I have shown you the perfect act of forgiveness and love. Forgive one another without limitations, without conditions. True forgiveness comes from knowing that God forgives any offense, however small or great it may be. Confront not those who have hurt you lest you hurt them in return. Instead, show love and mercy. Love is the key to the path to holiness. I have shown you the way, just follow Me.

[67] **April 11, 2017, Tuesday** (Prayer Room, 10:00 AM) Retaliation is not the answer to obtaining peace. If loving one another is truly not in your heart, how, then, do you expect to forgive? Be quick to ask for pardon even if you do not think you offended. Do not allow pride to creep in and hinder you from reconciliation. Be promoters of peace. Be the bearers of love. I look upon My children with love despite their burdens of sin. Ask Me to fill your heart with love so that pride will have no room. Come to Me and allow My light to crush pride at its heel. Do not be pretentious. Your true self must be visible to all. If you fill your heart with love, then love will be evident in all your

ways. But if you have pride and self-love, then they, too, will be visible to all. Which one would you rather others see? Which one would you like to take hold of your heart, your being? The ways of My followers are a contradiction to the dictates of the world. And because they live according to My will, they will serve as My light for others to follow. Come, take My hand. Follow Me. I will lead you home.

[68] April 12, 2017, Wednesday (Prayer Room, 1:00-3:00 PM) I was once human, too. At the peak of My ministry, I chose to spend time in prayer. I set aside time for My Father. Why, then, My dear children, do you not want to spend time with Me? I have shown you that I, the Son of the Living God, prayed. Why can you not? My children, if you only could see the graces that flow from Me to those who seek Me, you would not hesitate to be on your knees and pray. If only you could see the outpouring of My love to those who love Me in return. Oh, My children, why must you let Me suffer so? Oh, My little children, come to Me, for I thirst for your love. The glory of My kingdom is closer than you think. My Father's goodness is something you cannot fathom. Come to Me, all of you who want to share in My glory. My arms are waiting to enfold you. Come, My little lamb. Reflect on the Father's love. An earthly Father provides for all the needs of his children to make them comfortable and happy. In the same way, My Father wishes to provide his children with all that they need for eternal happiness. No earthly Father wants doom for his children. And just so, our Heavenly Father does not want His children in eternal damnation. Would you not want to spend eternity with someone who is the source of all good? Secure no goods from this world. But instead, gain spiritual goods. Be not satisfied with the fleeting happiness of this world, but seek true happiness that comes from true love. I'll tell you again, love. Conform not with the love the world offers, the shallow, love-lust kind. Ask the Father to fill you with the love that has no boundaries, no limitations, no conditions. This kind of love is the kind that can change the world. Forget the past and be in the present with Me. So many live in the past, are afraid of the future, and forget that I am present with them each day. I tell you again, I have forgotten the past, and only I know of your future. Why can you not enjoy today with Me? People choose to cloud themselves with the worries of tomorrow. Why not choose to clothe yourselves with My all-consuming love? Now is the time to change. Make a conscious effort to commune with Me daily. Intimacy is what I desire. If you only knew how close I am to you. So close yet ignored by so many. I am here. My child, I like spending time with you. I enjoy our conversations. I know it is difficult at times to believe that it is I speaking with you. I thank you for being open to My words. The time will come when I will reveal why I chose to come to you. For now, just marvel at the words I share with you. Do not concern yourself as to who to share them with. You have done well in choosing who to tell up to now. You have the grace to know beyond what you allow yourself to believe. Trust in the gifts I have bestowed on you. I have trusted you with these gifts. I know you will use them well. Again and again, I tell you, pursue holiness! Your heart is meant to love Me. Dear child, I love you so!

[69] April 13, 2017, Thursday (Prayer Room, 9:00-10:00 AM) Tenderness and compassion are manifestations of love. We created everyone with different traits and personalities, talents and gifts, strengths and weaknesses. All we ask is your forbearance with one another. Rejoice at each other's success.

Forgive each other's faults. Pardon each other's shortcomings. Love one another. Conduct yourselves with joy to attract the goodness in others' hearts. Kind words and actions can always dispel disputes. Love begets love. Peace begins with love. Look at everyone with compassion. In this way, it will be difficult to find fault in others. Seek the gentle path to disagreements, thus avoiding arguments among you. Do not allow the enemy to destroy relationships by using love as your armor. You see, love is always the answer. Forgive before you approach someone who has done you wrong. In this way, you already won. Humility is a great form of love. Defeat is not a sign of weakness; it is a great act of humility. I exalt My humble servants. Humility and love go together on the path to holiness. Take this road, and you will find Me. See Me in everyone. Would you argue and throw hateful words at Me? Would you ridicule Me? Would you purposely hurt Me? Remember that I suffer with each of My children. Would you add on to My suffering? Again, I ask you to love one another. It is love that can conquer the world. Be a blessing to others by bringing My love. My will is for you to be the guiding light for many. People are naturally attracted to goodness. Bring My lost sheep back to Me. Let them follow you. Direct them to Me, My child, for so many are lost. Do not be afraid, for I am always beside you. The path to Me is love. Come home to Me, My children. My eternal love awaits.

[70] **April 14, 2017, Good Friday** (Prayer Room, 8:00 AM) Counsel the doubtful. My death on the cross is a sacrifice for all My children across all generations. My Mercy has no end. Pray, My child, pray that all will know of My love for them. This new generation of minds that question My very existence fills Me with unbearable sorrow. I have already suffered for this

on the cross, and still, I continue to suffer. Console My heart with your prayers for all who have strayed away. They have fallen into the traps set by the enemy. So far gone that they cannot even say My name with reverence. Reach out to them with My salvific mission. Offer them love, for this can ignite fire into the darkness of hopelessness. My child, waste not any more time on idleness. Go beyond your reach, your comfort zone. Seek out those oppressed by worldly sins. What good does it do if you only go to those close to you? They already know Me. Go, find My lost sheep, go. Arm yourself with nothing but love. I will give you courage and boldness to proclaim the truth. Deaf ears will listen. Hardened hearts will melt at the words of hope. Stubborn minds will halt at the sound of My name whispered by the just. Why wait? The time is now. The war against the enemy has already begun. My humble servants, I need you. Heed the call of My Father. Heaven needs you.

[71] **April 15, 2017, Saturday** (Prayer Room, 8:00 AM) The message of hope will bring back many to My flock. Surrender to the will of My Father. Subdue the tendency to flee from favors I ask for. Though unseen, you can recognize My promptings. Just listen. You can hear My voice. The more time you spend with Me, the more you will know the ways I speak. Spark curiosity by your lives. Let God's love emanate from you. My faithful servants, your inner beauty will shine in the crowd. My lost sheep will be attracted by your light. Let your actions direct them back to Me. Just be willing to serve Me, and I will do the rest. Compromise not with the enemy. His false promises have lured My children to fall away. Rebuke every evil thought. Harbor only love, and you will have the strength of an army. Keep your focus on Me, your Savior.

(9:45 AM) Fill your heart with gladness, for I came and died for you. A joyful heart does not have room for doubt and fear. A heart brimming with love has no choice but to share it with others. Console the downtrodden, for all they need is love. Promote peace wherever we may lead you. The beauty of the just will outshine a room full of enemies. Your duty is to God, everything else comes after. How I delight in your obedience, My child. You are loved!

[72] **April 16, 2017, Easter Sunday** (Adoration Chapel, 11:30 AM) Give glory and praise to God alone! My sacrifice on the cross is for the salvation of all. Bring this good news to My children. Many have forgotten what I did for them. Many have rejected My offer of eternal happiness. Bring back to Me all who have forsaken Me. Be the one voice calling souls out of darkness. Be the one who contradicts the call of the world. I will let the voice of the just be heard. If it falls on deaf ears, move on, for many are waiting. Do not be afraid. I am with you always. Show forth God's goodness. Proclaim the message of salvation. Be bold and steadfast. The Holy Spirit is upon you. There is nothing to fear. My Mother's mantle protects Her faithful children. What more do you need? Pick up your cross with gladness, knowing that I am carrying it with you. The task ahead is lighter when we do it together. My child, you have nothing to fear. I am with you always. You are loved!

[73] **April 17, 2017, Monday** (Prayer Room, 10:30 AM) Place your trust in Me. I can make miracles happen. When you trust, the more you will see My goodness. If you let Me orchestrate your life, the more you appreciate the plans I have laid out for you. Avoid the tendency to over-plan. Resist this temptation so as not to take control from Me. Let go and submit to My will.

Do I not always take care of you? Again, I ask you to conform your will with Mine. The day may present hardships, pitfalls, joys, and sorrows. I know what is in your every day. If you keep your gaze at Me, if you hold My hand, you have nothing to be afraid of. Know, My child, that I am preparing you for an eternity with Me. If you allow Me to guide you, the journey will be less treacherous. Let Me lead the way. I can show you ways to avoid the traps of the enemy. Follow your Shepherd. I will take you home.

[74] **April 19, 2017, Wednesday** (Adoration Chapel, 9:45 AM) The promise of eternal salvation applies to all My children. See to it that all will know of our love for all. Although many have rejected us, we will never reject anyone. The transgressions of many will never alter our love for humanity. Our everlasting love transcends through all generations. A thankful heart gives us pure joy. Your obedience to My will pleases us so. See how opening your heart to Us changes your perspective in life. Rely on Me for all your needs. Submitting your will to Us opens doors that you never dreamed of. Taking control almost always closes many possibilities. Trust in My Divine Providence always. We can never be outdone in Our generosity. Persist in finding a time to meet with Me. Take Me through your day and allow Me to be your companion. I love being a part of your every day. My child, how I love you. You are precious in My sight.

[75] **April 20, 2017, Thursday** (Prayer Room, 10:00 AM) Learning to depend on Me is a hard task to master. Most people quit at the first test and go about their way. Patience and perseverance go together in any situation. In this world where people want instant resolution, waiting for My response to their prayers is almost always set aside for their solutions. Instead of

submitting to My will, My children choose to find their way out of the opportunity to learn a virtue. Help Me reach out to those who chose to close their doors on Me. Because of self-love, they have rejected God's love. Because of pride, they take control and forget to let Me steer them. They call on Us out of desperation, and still, they take the rein. My children, come to Me. I have all the answers to all your dilemmas. I have all the graces you need to face any trials set on the road home. Come to My Sacred Heart. The bounty that awaits the faithful is immeasurable. Why resort to human frailty when you have the strength of your Lord to depend on? My children, I am here. Call My name. Come to Me. Like a Father watching his child learn to walk, we, too, will let you fall. Do we leave you on the ground? No. We are always beside you, watching and guiding you, ready to lend a helping hand. Did you not crawl before you walked? Did you not take the time to learn a new skill? In the same way, allow Us to guide you and teach you the virtues needed on your journey home. Come to us. Your Father awaits.

[76] **April 21, 2017, Friday** (Prayer Room, 8:00 AM) Speak for Me. Allow the Holy Spirit to speak through you. I left My teachings for all to follow, but so few listened. Be My voice. You do not need to be a scholar to be heard. Your example of goodness, truth, and love can convert the hearts of many. Stay simple and pure. Those who are seeking Me will find light in you. Do not doubt My omnipotence. Am I not your God?

*interrupted, went to Mass

(10:30 AM) Surrender and receive. Do not allow human intellect to take control. Instead, allow Me to guide you in using your intelligence for the glory of God. Relying on your abilities does not always coincide with My plans. Submit your will to Us, and We will show you more ways to use your talents for the good of all. Let go of your worries. The more you cling to them, the more you cannot trust. Truly, I say to you, place your trust in Me. The enemy wants to weigh you down. Let Me lift you. Trust Me. My child, focus on today. Spend this day with Me. Be with Me.

[77] **April 22, 2017, Saturday** (Prayer Room, 3:00 PM) I see the desires of your heart. Self-love has taken control of most of My children's hearts. So many look inwardly for self-preservation. So many have neglected to look outward to their neighbors. How common has it become to turn the other way when others need help? A simple prayer for someone else has become a novelty. Oh, My dear children! What has happened to the human heart? I created you to be in union with Me, the source of all love. How I long for My children to love Me. How I long for you to love each other. This need for constant pleasure, personal well-being, and acceptance is always connived by the enemy to lure them away from Me. My children, open your heart to Me. Allow Me to transform you into the loving children you were meant to be. Each heartbeat is a gift from Me. Please love Me. My child, show love. Be love. Bring back to Me, My children, through your love. The more love you give, the more love I will fill your heart with. Come back to My Sacred Heart. All My children, come.

[78] **April 23, 2017, Divine Mercy Sunday** (Adoration Chapel, 11:00 AM) Today, I rejoice for My children bask in My mercy. How My heart swells with love for all who proclaim My mercy. Thank you, My children, for heeding My wishes. Although many still do not know of this special day, the prayers of the just ones flood the gates of heaven. What bounty awaits those who ask for mercy! Bring the message of mercy to the hopeless. My children,

there is nothing I cannot give you. There is nothing I cannot forgive. Come, come back to Me. My little ones, come. Keep the desire to love burning in your hearts. It is much easier to turn your back on sins of the flesh if you let love take over your soul. Do not hesitate, run to My bountiful mercy. I am here, ever present, ever waiting. Whatever I have forgiven has been forgotten. The past is in the past; leave it where it should be. Come then and live in the present with Me. I have said this before, and I say it once more: My mercy abounds for all My children. Ask for My mercy. Just ask and I will give. I desire to give My all and ask for nothing in return. Come, My children, your Father waits for your return home. My love overflows to all of you.

(St. Matthew Catholic Church, 3:00 PM) There is no sin too great that I cannot forgive, no transgressions that I cannot forget. My heart desires for all to receive My mercy. My children, you cannot comprehend yet the depths of My love. In the meantime, come so that the rays of My mercy can penetrate your souls. Remain open to receive, for I have so much to give. How I thirst for souls to turn to Me. I do not wish for any of My children to perish in the hands of the enemy. I desire for all My children to see Me in glory.

[79] **April 24, 2017, Monday** (Prayer Room, 8:00 AM) Surrendering your will to Mine should give you comfort instead of fear. Insisting on going about life your way only limits possibilities. Do you trust Me? It is through trust that would enable you to let go of your worries. You may not understand the circumstances in your life right now, but if you surrender to Me, I will show you how all the pieces fit together. Taking control of one's life always pushes Me away. I wish to be a part of your life.

Make Me a part of your day. Plan your day with Me, and then let Me show you what I have set for you. You see, My child, I take care of My flock. I am always looking out for you. Never do I take My glance off you. Do the same for Me. The path to Me is not so hard if you trust in Me. Do you see Me at work in your life? Do you feel My presence? I have intricately designed your every day to make you aware of Me. Again, see Me. Look beyond what you visually see and then perceive My handiwork for you, only you. How I love you, My child! You are so precious to Me!

[80] **April 25, 2017, Tuesday** (Prayer Room, 2:00 PM) Develop the habit of shutting off the world to spend time with Me. Make Me the priority of your day. In this way, you allow yourself to receive the graces you need for the day. I do not hold back My blessings. Just come to Me and ask. I wish to be intimate with all My children. What Father does not want to be a part of his children's lives? Let Me enter into your life. I am the Father of all. Join Me and the army of the faithful as we spread love. Plant seeds of hope and faith wherever you are to go. Find comfort in knowing that the Lord, your God, is orchestrating your life to center on love. Continue to be obedient to My call. My daughter, you please Me with your willingness to serve Me. I understand your concerns. Continue to surrender your will to Me. Changes are soon to come.

(4:00 PM) Remember this: the more you let go, the more you live. A life lived with Me opens graces you cannot fathom. Let Me live in you. Let Me be a part of you. Do not hold back anything from Me. Surrender and partake in My goodness. You are loved. Just be still and know that I am beside you.

[81] **April 26, 2017, Wednesday** (Prayer Room, 8:00 AM) Consider all the possibilities that I can open for you if you

surrender your will. I have many unopened doors that you did not allow Me to open for you in the past. Would you not want to see what I have prepared for you? Cling on to Me and not your ways. Persist in seeking My will, for I have many surprises for you. I am God. I am your Father. I am also your brother and friend. I am entitled to your utmost respect and reverence. At the same time, come to Me as your best friend. I take pleasure when My children talk to Me like I am a peer. I enjoy it when you approach Me in your most natural, human way. It is then that you make Me real in your life. That is how I live in you, with you, through you. Do you not enjoy My company? Come to Me, My child. Let the world vanish when we are together. I love you.

[82] **April 27, 2017, Thursday** (Prayer Room, 8:00 AM) Rejoice in the Lord! Jump in jubilation for the Lord; your God is with you! Sing praises to God. Fill your heart with joy. God is always at your side! So many of My children spend their days in gloom and dread. Why? If they knew how they are loved by God, they, too, would rejoice. My child, help My children. Conform your will to Mine. Together, let us conquer the world through love. The wave of sin has been crashing in the lives of My children. Help Me save them from drowning in their sins. Bring to them My love. Bring to them My words of hope and justice. Bring to them peace. Pave a new road for them, a road that leads to Me. Do not be afraid. I am always at your side. You do not have to make special plans. Just let Me take your hand and guide you. Keep your eyes on Me, keep your heart filled with love, and I will do the rest. Be My hands, My feet, My voice. Keep your mind open to My promptings. Do not busy yourself planning, studying, and preparing. Let Me work through you. Submit and be open to Me. My child, stay obedient to Me alone. Cast your

worries aside. I, the Lord, your God is in control. I love you, dear one. The Holy Spirit is with you.

(Bedroom, 5:49 PM) Join the angels in praising Me. That is all I need from you now. Take these moments to praise Me. I am preparing you for heavenly work. Just praise Me.

*The last entry was the answer when I asked the Lord who He wants Me to serve him as instructed by my spiritual director.

[83] **April 28, 2017, Friday** (Prayer Room, 10:30 PM) Develop a habit of thanking Me for everything. Acknowledging that I make all things happen, be it good or tragic, is a start at becoming aware of My presence in your life. Thank Me for...

*unfinished, too tired to continue.

[84] **April 29, 2017, Saturday** (Prayer Room, 4:30 PM) Today, fill your heart with thanksgiving. The Lord, your God, has blessed you! Look around you. The bounty of the Lord surrounds you. What is there before you are gifts from above? Accept everything with thanksgiving. Do not allow pride and envy to enter your souls. I, your Potter, mold each one of you differently. Do not compare your journey with any of My children. Each of you is loved the same way, but each has your path to travel. Praise Me. Thank Me. That is all I ask of you. Today, thank Me.

[85] **April 30, 2017, Sunday** (Prayer Room, 4:45 PM) Collect your thoughts. Your concerns are scattered in many places. Direct your thoughts to Me. Let Me help you in redirecting your focus on what is imperative. I have set this time aside for you to learn to rely on Me. Let go of the rein and let Me take the lead. Let Me be your guide. Let Me be your Father. Wait a little longer. Patience, My child, patience. I want you to enjoy this time with Me. Just spend time with Me as My child. You have a lifetime to

be My servant. For now, just be My child. Rest in My presence. Enjoy My company. My child, how I love you so!

MAY

"There are five excellent qualities which are required in all prayer.
A prayer must be confident, ordered,
suitable, devout and humble."
St. Thomas Aquinas

[86] May 3, 2017, Wednesday (Prayer Room, 7:00 AM)
Nothing can separate you from Me. Only the enemy can cause a rift between Us, but My mercy freely flows to those who come back to Me. Do not doubt My Omnipotence. There is nothing you want that I cannot give. Just remember that what you perceive as unanswered prayer can be My answer. All I want is for all My children to come home to Me. I only grant those prayers that will lead you home. Today, console Me with your love. I thirst for all to love Me in return. Whisper My name with love. Let your every breath be a profession of your love for Me. Just love Me. Destroy any unforgiving thought. Leave no room for hatred and envy in your heart. Malicious thoughts about others are directed to Me, as well. You are all My children. No Father would want anyone to ridicule or hurt his child. I feel the same way when any of My children are judged and offended. Fill your thoughts with love and goodness, and then the enemy will have no way to plant seeds of ruination. My daughter, teach about love. Live love. The more you show love to others, the more they will want to love. Comfort Me with your obedience to My will.

Show others how to love. Your Father in heaven waits for your return home.

[87] **May 4, 2017, Saturday** (Adoration Chapel, 1:00 PM) Today, console My Sacred Heart by whispering My Name with love. My Holy Name, used by so many without reverence but if said with love, brings forth many blessings. I, the Son of God, tremble in delight at the sound of My name tenderly spoken by My Mother. I wish for you to do the same. Let Me feel your love as you say My name. Dispel My sadness by calling out My name with love. Continue to trust and surrender. See how I open the doors to those who patiently wait and persevere. I am well pleased by your gratitude and openness to My will. When you wait patiently without any expectations, you allow Me to carry out My will freely. How I wish all My children would do the same! Having preconceived ideas and plans only creates disappointments and, at times, bitterness. Give Me your complete trust. I will not let you down. Participate in My work of salvation by bringing My love to others. Just as the apostles went out to foreign lands, take only My burning love for all humankind. You do not need any special skills or experience. All you need is love for God. The Holy Spirit is always guiding you. He is all you need. My child, continue to stay attentive to Me. Learn as I teach you ways to detach from the world. Your focus should be on Me alone. Listen, My child, listen. I have so much more to say. Stay humble and vigilant. I am always with you. You are loved.

[88] **May 5, 2017, Friday** (Prayer Room, 11:00 PM) Be still, My child. Just rest in My presence. It has been a long day. Thank you for singing to Me today. Those moments I treasure forever. Rest now.

[89] May 6, 2017, Monday (Prayer Room, 7:00 PM) Guard against any pretense. Hypocrisy is, in essence, lying to God, to others, and oneself. Keep in mind that We can see through you. Work on keeping your soul beautiful in the eyes of God. Let your love of God be reflected in everything that you do. Be who you are with God and with others. Look not at how other people perceive you but at how God sees you. In everything, be truthful.

[90] May 7, 2017, Tuesday (Prayer Room, 7:00 AM) Return to Me, not half-heartedly, but completely. I wish to be in union with not just a part of your heart and soul but the whole of you. I wish for you to have no other gods but Me alone. How I long to take you home. No words are fitting to describe the beauty and bounty in the Paradise I have prepared for all My children. Return to Me, and I will walk with you in Paradise. Take care not to get swayed by others' opinions. [Follow Deacon Bill's direction. I, too, speak to him.] Your main concern should be in maintaining your trust in Me. Go about your duties without much thought about your ministry. Always remember that My timing is always perfect. Do not complicate matters by taking them into your hands. Give God, the Father, the glory by allowing Him to take control. Just be My willing lamb, and I will take you home. Do not be discouraged if the enemy sends you opposition. Good works are always a threat to Satan. Again, be vigilant and pray incessantly. I will protect you. My Mother protects you. Choirs of angels are always at your side to protect you. Joseph, my foster father, protects you. My Archangel Michael has always been your protector. There is nothing to fear. You are not alone. Distribute My messages to all. There is no need to divulge what is transpiring in your life at the time of My messages. My words alone can change the hearts of many. Honor

My wishes, My child. Your obedience is what I wish for. Just be patient. You are loved.

Recall to mind when you started on this journey. You came to Me with an open mind and heart, not knowing what to expect. You were silent and waited patiently for My words. Now that You have learned how to listen, I want to teach you how to speak My words. In the same way, I want you to wait patiently when the time comes for you to speak for me. There is no need for much preparation. Just come again with an open heart and mind. Wait and see. Do you love Me? Let your love for Me continue to grow. See how the world vanishes when you are in complete union with Me. [That is where you were after communion today. You were so in tune with Me that you lost track of everything else but Me.] Continue to immerse yourself in My presence, and I will take you places. Your obedience pleases Me. I love you, My dear one! I love you! Sharing My words to others is of utmost importance. Do not dwell on how you are to proceed. My child, let go of the rein! No amount of planning on your part can change the course of events in your life. Only I know of the path you are to take. Take every day with an open mind. Keep gazing only at Me. Worry not about tomorrow! Practice the art of surrendering to Me alone. Complex plans and actions can only hinder My work. You will see how simple your work is if you learn to give up your desire to take control. I hear your concerns and worries. Offer them all to Me. There is no need to foresee what is to come. Just be present with Me and, with eager anticipation, see what I will do. Trust Me.

(Adoration Chapel, 8:35-8:52 PM) Do not fall into the trap of comparing yourself to My children, who also have received special graces. We have set you apart for a different ministry, a different purpose. Stay obedient to My will and wait as We unfold Our plans for you. My child, I need you. Heaven needs your work on earth for the glory of the Father. Wait and see.

[91] **May 8, 2017, Monday** (Adoration Chapel, 12:50-12:55 PM) Come with Me then, My child, to our special tree. Come and sit with Me under its shade. You and I, in peace. Feel the gentle breeze. Listen to the leaves as they sway from the soft wind. Lay your head on My shoulder. Rest, My child. Rest your sleepy head. How wonderful it is to spend time with you. I will stay as long as you wish. Just you and Me.

[92] **May 9, 2017, Tuesday** (Prayer Room, 9:20 PM) Dear little one, stay with Me. Come meet Me every day and spend time with Me. How happy you make Me feel with your imagination. Yes, someday, we will be together in the place you imagine us to be. I promise. Continue to have a joyful heart despite what others may think of as adversities. I see how you are handling your current medical situation. It pleases Me that you have a peaceful disposition. You're a very trusting lamb. Continue to surrender. Rest now, My child. I look forward to meeting with you tomorrow. Rest now.

[93] **May 10, 2017, Wednesday** (Prayer Room, 8:50 AM) Deep in the recesses of each one's heart is a desire to love God. Ignite that desire in My children's hearts. Still, I long for My children to love Me. Capture the hearts of many by your example. Show others how to love by your words and actions. Great intellectuals who have the knowledge and expertise on many things can never explain love. Show them what love is. The path to Me is easy. Just follow love. When you look at everything in the world with love, suddenly, the path becomes clear. Your neighbor, who has always

been annoying you, will seem different to you. The boss with whom you have so much distrust would be seen in a different light. The person who has always shown you disapproval would become less of a threat. Love is the key. Love is the center of peace. Love is the way to Me. Do not turn away from those in need. Disregard any malicious thoughts or question other's intent. Pray to expel any evil influence on them. I see your intention. Let love guide you. Plant seeds of hope and love as you minister to My children.

(12:07 PM) Foster friendships with those who have turned their back on My Church. Break down barriers with your joy. You see, My child, the more you love Me, the more My light will shine through you. The time will come when My children will return in great numbers. Be ready to welcome them. Go now to prepare for your journey. Be open to My promptings. Listen and follow My will. My dearest daughter, how I love you so!

[94] May 11, 2017, Thursday (Adoration Chapel, 11:30 PM) As you embark on a new journey, I want you to trust in Me. Be at peace, for I am guiding you. Many things are hidden from you now. I hear your questions; I know your thoughts. You have done what I have asked you to do for now. Let go and trust. Be an obedient servant. Do not go before your Master. All will be revealed in due time. Continue to be attentive to Me. You will know what you are to do when it is time. My child, fret not. Cast your worries aside. Cherish each today and now. Each moment is a gift from Me. There is no need to search for Me. I have never left your side. Keep Me company, for I am always with you. My child, go forth. You are blessed.

[95] May 15, 2017, Monday (Adoration Chapel, Our Lady of Mount Carmel of St. Joseph, Lucena City, Philippines 6:10 AM)

Delve into the depths of My Sacred Heart by learning how to love. Follow the footsteps of the saints who didn't just stop at loving; they were perfect examples of love. My children, I ask you to love. Bitterness and hatred, remove from your hearts. How can I dwell in your soul if it is darkened by pride and unforgiveness? Heed My plea, for I wish to live in your hearts. Persist in doing My will. Be attentive now. I do want you to cherish your time with your family, but I want you to keep watch. Keep holding My hand. Trust in Me. Allow the Holy Spirit to work through you. My sweet lamb, continue to be obedient. I am leading the way.

[96] **May 16, 2017, Tuesday** (Lucena City, Philippines, 11:00 AM) Be still and be at peace. Find comfort in knowing that I only ask for your obedience. The path to holiness entails many tests designed to strengthen your reliance on Me. Resolve to crush the temptation to balk at challenging tasks. I have already opened many doors for you because you obey. Trust in Me.

[97] **May 18, 2017, Thursday** (Manila, Philippines, 7:00 AM) Place your trust in Me. Do not dwell so much on what might come. Accept all that I place in your hands. Remember that I already have prepared you for this task. Wait a little longer. Console My heart by your trust. A worrisome attitude does not lead to trust. Be at peace. I am always working for your good. The hearts of many will be stirred by My words. In due time, these words will get to them. Keep your faith in Me. Trust in Me. Be at peace. I am always at your side. I love you, My little lamb. You are precious in My sight. Go about your day knowing that I am with you.

[98] **May 20, 2017, Saturday** (Lucena City, Philippines, 7:00 AM) Remove any lingering doubt. Am I not your Shepherd?

Trust Me, I continue to lead you despite the passing of time. Patience, My child. Your journey continues. Profess your love for Me to all you encounter. My children have forsaken Me. Be a reminder to them that I still exist, that I still love. Bring back My lost sheep. My child, gather My children, for I wish nothing less than to spend an eternity with all. Thank Me for everything. Silence on My part does not mean abandonment. Trust that all your prayers are being heard. With an open heart, accept Our response. Live according to Our will and be at peace. My child, continue to take Me wherever you go. Continue to call My name. You please Me so!

[99] **May 21, 2017, Sunday** (Lucena City, Philippines, 7:00 AM) Sing praise to God. Give God the glory. Offer Him Thanksgiving for His blessings. Praise your God, your Creator. Let your heart soar with joyful worship for the Lord, Your God, loves you. Unite your souls with your Heavenly Father. Sing praise to God alone. Offer your thoughts and prayers for the salvation of the humankind. My children are too weak to resist the temptations of the world. They are perishing at the hands of the enemy. Gather them, My child. Lead them back to Me. I need more hands and feet to work in My vineyard. Gather the workers. I will send them your way. Teach and guide them to propagate the faith. Do not be afraid. Persist in doing what is good. Despite the noise, you will hear Me. Trust that I make all things happen for a reason. Just trust Me. I will never forsake you. My little lamb, I love you.

[100] **May 22, 2017, Wednesday** (Adoration Chapel, Our Lady of Mount Carmel of St. Joseph, Lucena City, Philippines, 6:20 AM) My child, continue to pray for Monsignor Castro. He is My servant at heart. I desire your trust and obedience. Be at

peace, for I am at work. Be still and wait. Be at peace. Jump not to conclusions. Only I can see what is in My children's hearts. Steer away from judging others. Remember that you are all My children. It is I who you persecute, I, you judge. Forgive one another. Be the light bearer of peace.

[101] May 26, 2017, Friday (Adoration Chapel, Our Lady of Mount Carmel of St. Joseph, Lucena City, Philippines, 6:15 AM) Sing to Me, My child. Sing praises! Words of love I long to hear from My children. Sing Me praises! Proclaim My goodness to all. Too few of My children have heard My call. Be My voice. Call them back to My flock. Too much time has been wasted. Pluck My children from their worldly stupor. Bring them back to Me. I will stir the heart of Monsignor Castro to complete his duty. Do not worry. My work continues despite what you perceive as inactivity. Continue to receive My words. I have much more to say. Visit Me frequently. I long for your company. (7:30 AM After Mass Feast of Saint Philip Neri) Let the truth always prevail. Using a pen name to hide your identity may seem to be the answer at this time. You will have to reveal our relationship to many eventually to allow others to follow in your footsteps. How are you to guide My children to better their faith if they cannot find you? My dear child, I wish for you to be available to those whom I will be sending your way. You are to build Me an army of disciples. Your anonymity is of the least importance in your role. You, My child, are to lead many souls back to Me. Do not worry; I am here to protect you and your family. Your willingness to serve Me brings Me so much joy. A servant's heart is frequently not attained by those who may show devotion to Me. Many cannot move from loving Me to knowing and serving Me because they refuse to give their whole selves to Me. Self-love is more prevalent than self-giving. Why, My children, oh why must you cling on to this world when you are all destined to be with Me? Oh, My dearest children, come back to Me! Holiness cannot be achieved by just being physically present at Mass. My graces cannot flow to those living in mortal sin. If only they know of the gifts I have waiting to bestow on them upon their return. My child, teach your brothers and sisters of the vileness of sins. Tell them of My Mercy. The wrath of My Father I would not wish on anyone. Like Him, I wish for all to return to the flock. It is not selfish to want Me for yourself. Love should consume your heart with the overwhelming desire to be united with Me. This is a grace I bestow to those who have entrusted their lives to Me and who have completely surrendered their souls to Me. Continue to please Me with your love. How I love you so!

[102] **May 29, 2017, Monday** (Lucena City, Philippines, 4:00 PM) I can see all pretenses. Remember that We can see through man's hearts. No amount of charitable work can cover up one's sins. I would rather see one act of love done in secrecy by a pure heart. Repent! Return to Me before it is too late. Do not delay. Conform your will with Mine. I cannot be outdone in generosity. I pour graces upon those who surrendered to My will. My children, come to Me with trusting hearts. There is nothing I cannot do for you, nothing that I cannot give. All I ask is that you surrender your will to Me completely. Events in your life are subtle teaching moments. Eternal happiness is gained through perseverance. Faith, hope, and charity are obtained by going through trust tests. Am I your only God? Do you have confidence in Me? Will you hand over the reign to Me? Can you hear Me calling you to love? I wish for you to rest your weary

mind. Take this time to rest from worldly cares. Your work has not begun. I need your complete attention once I set things in motion. Let your guard down. I am giving you rest. Do not deny Me the chance to be intimate with you. Moments like this are precious to Me. My child, I want you home with Me. I, too, long to spend an eternity with you. I love you!

[103] May 31, 2017, Wednesday (Lucena City, Philippines, 3:00 PM) Do not let tomorrow trouble you. Ponder on what I have set before you today. Each day comes with many opportunities to serve Me. You need not go to foreign lands to minister to My children. Everyone around you is My child, too. Your family needs you. You have wisdom beyond your years, harness this gift for the good of all. As you tend to My children, do not let their sins cloud your attitude towards them. You are to show mercy as I have shown you, My mercy. Again, do not judge. I created all My children out of love. Everyone can love. My sweet child, show love. [You have shown Me great trust in this mission. Thank you, My dear one. I will soon reveal more details. There is no need to think of specifics. All your questions will be answered soon.] Just as I have inspired you, your children will also receive guidance from the Holy Spirit. Continue to lead them closer to Me. They are all very special to Me. Like you, they have special roles in the ministry. Encourage your whole family to be in full communion with Me. Special graces are waiting for all of them upon their return to My table. Your willingness to serve Me has gained you many graces for your family. Bring them all back to Me. Bring back to Me more souls. Yes, I am most pleased by his (My husband's) change of heart. This was meant to be. Like him, your example of love and faith in Me will stir many hearts. The Holy Spirit is at work in you. Do not hinder his work by hesitation. Listen and be attentive to his promptings. My child, you please Me so.

[104] May 31, 2017, Wednesday (Our Lady of Guadalupe Church, Sariaya, Quezon, Philippines, 7:00 PM) TAGALOG: Gagabayan kita sa lahat ng landas na iyong tatahakin. Huwag kang magambala. Hinubog na kita. Masdan mo ang mukha ng aking Ina. Balang araw makakamtam mo din na makita siya. Ipagbunyi mo ang Ama sa Langit. TRANSLATION: I will guide you on all the roads that you will travel. Do not be troubled. I have formed you. Look at the face of My Mother. One day you, too, will see Her. Give praises to the Father in Heaven.

JUNE

*"Those who say they don't have time for prayer,
are not lacking time, but love."*
St. John Paul II

[105] June 2, 2017, Friday (Adoration Chapel, Our Lady of Mount Carmel of St. Joseph, Lucena City, Philippines, 11:00 AM) Do you love Me? Do you trust Me? Can you see yourself living an eternity with Me? My sweet child, I can see your impatience. There's nothing more for you to do but wait. You have been obedient to the promptings of the Holy Spirit. [Let Him do His work.] Spend time with Me. Adore Me. Love Me. This is the time for you to rest and listen. My sweet little lamb, trust in Me. The wall of the convent protects those who have consecrated themselves to Me from the noise of the world. In the same way, I ask you to build up protective barriers from the influence of the world through prayers. Always start your day in prayer and ask for the shield of faith. Arm yourself with the graces that I bestow each time you pray. Come to Me in prayer and allow Me to spend each day with you. My Mother has the power to crush the head of the serpent. Seek Her intercession. She is your Mother, too. This ever-changing world is going farther away from Me. Help Me gather those who still believe, who still have faith in Me. Strengthen their desire and respond to the call to be My disciples. I have planted the desire in their hearts. Help Me call out to them. This mission will stir their love for Me. From love will flow the desire to serve. Help pave the way for My children to reconcile with Me. Part of the problem is the non-recognition of sins plotted by Satan's lies. Unveil sins. Spread the truth in the Gospels. Help remove the scales in My children's eyes so they can see how far away they have turned from Me. Unmask Satan and all his lies. Glorify the Father by bringing souls back to Him. Dear children, come back to Me.

[106] **June 4, 2017, Sunday** (Lucena City, Philippines, 7:00 AM) Profess your love for Me. I thirst for My children's love. How I long to hear words of love and thanksgiving from My children. Instead, all I hear are supplications for material things. Seldom do We hear praise and adoration. Oh, My children, I can give you everything you are asking for. But first, will you give up your other gods? Will you surrender your will to Me? Will you get to know Me? Will you love Me? Come to Me, My children. I am waiting. Attend to the needs of your family. As you minister to them, you serve Me as well. Pay attention to what I have set before you each day. You have permitted Me to be in control. Let Me do My work while you do yours. Pay attention. You have other opportunities to serve besides the mission. My child, be patient. I love you.

Don't miss out!

Visit the website below and you can sign up to receive emails whenever Barbara Valmeo publishes a new book. There's no charge and no obligation.

https://books2read.com/r/B-A-RTRK-QCMFB

BOOKS 2 READ

Connecting independent readers to independent writers.

About the Author

Barbara Valmeo, a dedicated wife, nurturing mother, devoted daughter, and caring sister, began receiving divine messages from the Lord in August 2016. Prompted by a Catholic seminarian, in the serene setting of the Adoration Chapel with pen and paper in hand, she fervently beseeched the Lord, echoing the words of 1 Samuel 3:10, "Speak, Lord, for your servant is listening." Having been nurtured in faith by devout Catholic parents, Barbara had always harbored a deep desire to serve the Lord as ardently as her parents had. Over the course of 20 years, she immersed herself in various ministries within her parish, discovering her profound passion for teaching and eloquent public speaking. Her inspiring talks, enlightening Bible studies, and guidance for both children and adults on matters of faith reflected her unwavering commitment to knowing, loving, and serving God, drawing inspiration from the lives of the Blessed Mother and numerous saints. This book encapsulates the profound revelations she has received from Jesus. Out of obedience, she shares the intimate dialogues she has with the Lord in her inner room (Matthew 6:6). Within its pages, readers will also gain insight into her daily life, experiencing her joys and struggles as a devoted homemaker and a nurturing homeschooling mom. Barbara's life journey had its roots in the Philippines before she embarked on a new chapter in the U.S. to pursue a career in Occupational Therapy in 1991. Married to Ysmael for 24 years, she made the heartfelt decision to leave her professional endeavors to raise their three children in Virginia. It is Barbara's sincere aspiration that those who peruse this book will be inspired to seek solace in their inner room, yearn for the heart of God, and hearken to His voice.